Praises for "Life's Little College A

Cole and Eric give you the best advice fr[...] [...] or the best college admission people in the country. Get it before you decide.

> Matthew Lesko
> New York Times Times best selling author

This book is the absolute best "first read" that anyone conducting a responsible collegiate search must have. This book strips away the complexities of many overwhelming decisions that seem daunting when college bound students and their parents begin the process. Once you read this book, you won't look at the college search the same ever again. Besides getting the same advice the countries top counselors would give their own children, Cole and Eric bring to life a very endearing story of family and a process that is clearly fun for them. A must read!

> Glenn Pere
> Founder
> CollegeClickTV.com

Making the best decision about college means getting the best possible information. wonderful book for both student and parents. I certainly could have used it when my three children and I went through the tedious process of selecting the right college, and most importantly, getting accepted!

Who better to write this book than a bright high-school senior and her father. Congratulations to Cole and Eric on a job well done.

A much needed and delightfully written book.

> Robert L. Shook
> New York Times best selling author

An incredibly useful resource! I wish I'd had this book when I was applying to college and I'm thrilled to have this information for when my own sons go through the admissions process.

Liz Elting
President & CEO
TransPerfect

Life's Little College Admissions Insights

Top Tips From the Country's Most Acclaimed Guidance Counselors

Eric and Cole Yaverbaum

New York

Life's Little College Admissions Insights
Top Tips From the Country's Most Acclaimed Guidance Counselors

Softcover ISBN: 978-1-60037-728-0

Hardcover ISBN: 978-1-60037-729-7

Library of Congress Control Number: 2009939756

MORGAN · JAMES
THE ENTREPRENEURIAL PUBLISHER

Morgan James Publishing
1225 Franklin Ave., STE 325
Garden City, NY 11530-1693
Toll Free 800-485-4943
www.MorganJamesPublishing.com

In an effort to support local communities, raise awareness and funds, Morgan James Publishing donates one percent of all book sales for the life of each book to Habitat for Humanity. Get involved today, visit **www.HelpHabitatForHumanity.org.**

Table of Contents

Dedication

To Wylie: We miss you at every single milestone not shared. Forever in our hearts.

And to Steph, John, and Max: And like you, every day in between.

Acknowledgements

We both can't thank my wife and childhood best friend, Suri Nisker (also known as Cole's mom), enough. She always talked to Cole (and me) as we went through the search process this past year, but was not able to travel with us to each of the colleges and universities we visited, so we were a little pulled apart by an illness that we all refuse to let interfere with our family being a family. She's a hero to both of us. You'll see in Cole's college essay on page 161 just what I mean.

Without Tenzin Chodon, we could not function as well as we do as a family. For almost 10 years, she has been our rock. She is a gift to us.

We also thank Cole's 11-year-old brother, Jace. What a trooper. He traveled to a lot more colleges and universities than your average 11-year-old does, and he loved every second of it! He proudly wears tee shirts from the schools he visited.

We thank our extended family, who had to hear a little more about the college search process than they might have liked because we were doing this book. They all enthusiastically listened and enjoyed, but we especially thank my co-author's beaming grandparents, Harry and Gayle Yaverbaum and Bernie and Noreen Nisker, who gave us their own wisdom as we went through the process.

My entire generation of our family is literally as proud of Cole as they would be if she were their own daughter. We are eternally grateful to Dana and David Zais, Merrill Nisker and Connie Oper, Lori Yaverbaum and Michael Berman, and Craig Nisker and Mona Holmes-Nisker. She is yours, too.

And we thank the next generation, always seeming like a little brother and sister to Cole, Remy and Logan Zais.

We are very grateful to the many college admission officers all over the country who gave us their advice. We spoke to hundreds of advisors who graciously gave us their time and wisdom, knowing that we would not be able to include them all in the book. While some were not included, every single advisor we spoke to helped us personally with our own education as we went through the process. We'll always be thankful for their time.

I'm very appreciative of my wise friends in the companies in which I'm a partner. They respect what it takes to be an author. I'm sincerely thankful to my associates for two decades, Mark DiMassimo, Lee Goldstein, Raul Vasquez, and Glenn Pere.

My agency and the great marketers we work with across the country always suffer from me having a little less time available while I am writing a book. I deeply appreciate the respect they showed for the time I spent writing yet another book.

I wish I could list everyone who deserves thanks here, but that would be a book in and of itself. A very big thank you to Felicitas Pardo, Danielle Nacco, Fern Marcya Edison, Kelly Duque, Mary Clare Jensen, Lauren Hovey, Jason Berger, Jenna Rosen, Jon Marshall, Ilana Abel, Dawn Becker, Andrea Biggs,

Jason Brownley, Haley Rubin, Ama Intsiful, Stephanie Tudor, Arielle Fisse, Daisy Murillo, Danielle Pieri, Thom Griffin, Natalie Borneo, Tara Pagan, Tara Runkle, Colleen Reasoner, Linnea Barone, Weno Gaseitsiwe, Christine Wolstenholme, Juanita Martinez, Ashley Vienna, Bill Fitzgerald, Cameron Frantz, Chris Carlberg, Dayna Sanders, Desiree Cortez, Gina Sund, Iva Zugic, Ivan Corsa, Jamie Korsen, Jennifer Yancey, Justin Prichard, John Patrick Robertson, Livan Grijalva, Marilyn Marsh, Margot Vaughan, Raymond Yip, Ruth Ayres, and Steve Dolan.

And finally, thanks to you, Cole, for letting me share a book cover with you.

Foreword

As my college-bound daughter and our family went through what often seemed like an overwhelming process of researching, visiting, applying to, and, finally, choosing the school that she felt was best for her, we learned so much. What seemed so complex at the beginning of the process seems much easier once you've been through it once. I find myself repeatedly saying, "If I had only known then what I know now..." just about every day.

That's why we wrote this book. We compiled this information in "real time" as we went through the college search as a family. We just finished what you may just be starting, and this book is intended to be a "jump starter" for you to use before you pick up even one of the many wonderful college directories and guides on the market today. The experts we talked to have different, and sometimes contrary, opinions on what's important, but they have some terrific and simple words of wisdom based on their experiences guiding so many. We hope you'll use this book in conjunction with a school guidance counselor, peer, parent, or expert who is helping you through the process, even if that "expert" is your own gut instinct.

While many adults look back on their college years as the best time of their life, nobody ever seems to say the same about the college application and selection process. So, our goal is to help make the search process as enjoyable and easy as possible. Now that we've come to the end of our own search, I'm thrilled that my co-author is going to have a great college experience herself beginning next year, and I can't wait to do this again with my son in six years! Enjoy the search.

Eric Yaverbaum

Introduction

Rising education costs, a deteriorating economy, and a rigorous admissions process make the college search process anything but simple. Since we spend a pivotal four years of our lives in college, it makes sense that we invest a great deal of time and care in the search for the perfect place (which we may find doesn't even exist). As of this writing, I'm searching for a college myself, and I've learned that much of the process is rife with uncertainty and is completely uncontrollable. But, here's the good news: other parts of the process can indeed be controlled by the applicants themselves.

Knowing when and how to start your search is essential. Organization is crucial. Without this knowledge and skill, the whole process can be overwhelming and, ultimately, disappointing. But with a little insight into the minds of guidance counselors—who are charged specifically with advising students with regard to college—the process suddenly becomes clear.

So what's the secret? How can you better understand the admissions process and the steps that precede it? By reading this book. We're giving you the inside scoop, the stuff they don't tell you on campus tours or in info sessions. Selecting a college is never going to be an easy process, but it doesn't have to be arduous, either.

Cole Yaverbaum
Class of 2014

Together, we're going to find the way for you to *enjoy* this process.

Ronna Morrison
Independent Educational Consultants Association
Ronna Morrison Associates
Demarest, New Jersey

CHAPTER ONE

What is one college tip that nobody ever seems to know?

Do not visit your first college choice first. Students should save the first choice for somewhere in the middle or for the last visit, so they have many other schools to compare it to before visiting their first choice.

Robert Bardwell
Secondary-Level Vice President, American School Counselor Association
President, New England Association for College Admission Counseling
School Counselor and Director of Guidance & Student Support Services
Monson High School
Monson, Massachusetts

In order to qualify for need-based financial aid, you need to fill out the FAFSA. You should file prior to February 15th.

Valerie Simmons, MEd
School Counselor
Pennsylvania

Most colleges will host students for an overnight visit once they are accepted. This really helps you decide if a college is right for you and reduces the likelihood of a transfer.

Cristiana M. Quinn, MEd
College Admission Advisors, LLC
Providence, Rhode Island

Don't follow the "you never know" philosophy of the college admissions process. Translated, that means: don't apply to a lot of colleges you know are beyond your reach.

Betsy Sherwood
Guidance Counselor
Tappan Zee High School
Orangeburg, New York

College should not be a competition, but a match.

Deborah Hardy, EdD
Chairperson of Guidance and Counseling Department
Irvington School District
Irvington, New York

Make your "name" your email address for college communication.

Jeannie Borin, MEd
President
College Connections
Encino, California

Pay attention to the guidelines colleges offer as to what kind of student they are looking for. No one seems to anticipate that terrible feeling one gets when reading the "denied" letters. It is painful.

Betsy Sherwood
Guidance Counselor
Tappan Zee High School
Orangeburg, New York

The students who do the right things are going to get the admission and scholarship offers—there is no "fate" or personal validation built into the college admissions process, no points for suffering in silence.

Keith Berman, CEP
President
Options for College, Inc.
New York, New York

Students should have eight first choices. Prioritizing before you get in closes minds.

Joyce Slayton Mitchell
Author
8 First Choices: An Expert's Strategies for Getting into College
College Advice U.S.A.
New York, New York

Thank your admissions rep. After a visit, go "old school" and send a handwritten postcard from your hometown/state, thanking them for their time. What's old is new again.

Robert F. Kennedy
Counselor/Post-Grad Coordinator
Smoky Hill High School
Aurora, Colorado

Ask for an appointment to interview with a human being and tour the college. Bring along items that make you unique to show off: portfolios of your articles, poems, songs, awards, speeches. Make sure you're one candidate for admission they won't forget! Then follow up with a note of appreciation.

Livia Sklar
Guidance Counselor
Bronx Aerospace Academy High School
Bronx, New York

Colleges do not like to admit students who are unlikely to attend. They make assumptions about strong students who express no interest in a school whatsoever. If a student has not communicated with a school at all except to apply there, they may not get in, even if their statistics are way above what the college is looking for.

Betsy Sherwood
Guidance Counselor
Tappan Zee High School
Orangeburg, New York

CONTACT! Make contact with the colleges you are really serious about.

Nathan J. Heltzel
School Counselor
Briarcliff High School
Briarcliff Manor, New York

Admissions officers aren't looking for reasons to reject you. They're looking at your application and trying to get comfortable with the idea of accepting you.

Scott Shrum
Co-Author
Your MBA Game Plan:
Proven Strategies for Getting into the Top Business Schools
Director of MBA Admissions Research
Veritas Prep
Malibu, California

For a variety of reasons, students don't take advantage of the summer and often regret the lost opportunity when the rush of activities kicks in at the start of the school year. Reminding students at the end of the school year about the benefits of using the summer months can go a long way towards alleviating major stress in the fall.

William Slocum
Guidance Counselor
Lenape High School
Medford, New Jersey

The college search process is NOT supposed to be a damaging experience. Create a list of schools that includes reaches, targets, and safeties, with a heavy hand on the safeties.

-Betsy Sherwood
Guidance Counselor
Tappan Zee High School
Orangeburg, New York

Students in the creative and performing arts don't seem to know that they can request to take a music lesson or a dance class or whatever class that relates to whatever they plan to study in the arts when they visit a college or university. Of course, they have to request this in advance of their visit.

Judy Zodda
Zodda College Services
Framingham, Massachusetts

Parents and students who do speak and get everything out on the table have the best perspective on things and fare the best in the process, without question; their stress levels are exponentially lower and they end up making the best decisions.

Philip M. Kavanagh
District Director of Guidance and Counseling
Lakeland Central School District
Shrub Oak, New York

A great time to take a subject test is after an AP exam.

Mandee Adler
Founder and Principal
International College Counselors
Hollywood, Florida

If financial aid is a concern for a family, then they should be investigating how each college handles financial aid before choosing a college. For example, most families assume that the expected family contribution number from the FAFSA will be the amount that they will be expected to pay. However, this is only true for those colleges that provide 100% of need. Most colleges do not provide this level of financial aid and instead practice "gapping," whereby they only give the student a certain percentage of their need. By focusing on colleges that provide more financial aid, the student can save thousands of dollars each year.

Todd Johnson
College Admissions Partners
Minnetonka, Minnesota

The one thing that parents and students forget is that there are more than 3,500 colleges in the US and there is more than one perfect college for a child.

Emilie Hinman
Dunbar Educational Consultants
New Canaan, Connecticut

Private colleges can potentially be equally as affordable as public options, depending on financial and merit-based aid.

Kiersten A. Murphy, MEd
Murphy College Consultants, LLC
Seattle/Bellevue, Washington

You are the customer, not the school.

Kristina L. Dooley
Independent Educational Consultant
Estrela Consulting
São Paulo, Brazil

College admission officers are usually very skilled at "reading" students, so do not think of the college admission process as a game and try to fake your interest in the school.

Marilyn G.S. Emerson, MSW, CEP
Independent Educational Consultants Association
College Planning Services, Inc.
Chappaqua, New York

When you've got your first short list of colleges, decide on your number one choice. If it isn't on Common App, then write the essay first. While Common App is your friend, not all colleges use it and if that is the case, you need to decide what your top choices are to focus your admissions questions appropriately.

Elisabeth Marksteiner
College Counselor & Alumni Relations
International School of Zug and Luzern
Zug, Switzerland

Colleges are looking for good citizens as well as good scholars. I try to impress upon my students the importance of ensuring that the colleges know something about your character as well as your SATs.

Don Dietrich
Director of College Guidance
Tower Hill School
Wilmington, Delaware

College admission officers need to "feel the love." Don't just tell them by applying early action, show them by multiple contacts!

Nathan J. Heltzel
School Counselor
Briarcliff High School
Briarcliff Manor, New York

It is ok to use "I" in your college essay.

Kiersten A. Murphy, MEd
Murphy College Consultants, LLC
Seattle/Bellevue, Washington

The biggest issue we struggle with is the misinformation from other parents who think they know what is going on and are not that informed.

Keith Elmore
Counselor for Gifted Students
Liberty High School
Liberty, Missouri

College is not a "bumper sticker" or a "sweatshirt" game, but the next journey in life to prepare for the global workforce.

Deborah Hardy, EdD
Chairperson of Guidance and Counseling Department
Irvington School District
Irvington, New York

Begin the process of self-discovery earlier than the summer/fall before senior year. The educational planning process takes time and more often than not, the process evolves over the course of that time. Waiting until the last minute to fill out applications makes for weak decisions in the college decision-making and college-planning processes.

Jean Marie Buckley, MEd, MPA
Founder and President
Buckley Educational Group, LLC
Burlingame, California

If you are considering a college that has tough admission standards, consider applying to a less competitive school your freshman year and transferring to the more competitive school later during your college career. Most highly competitive colleges admit a higher percentage of students after the frenzy of freshman year. Remember, it's not where you start your college education that employers ask you about, it's where you finish your degree.

Jennifer Muffick
School Counselor
J.I. Case High School
Racine, Wisconsin

Be your child's "clerical concierge." Make a file box before freshman year. Quietly collect everything your kid will otherwise lose: standardized test results, transcripts, sports awards, community-service hours.

Kris Hintz
Owner
Position U 4 College, LLC
New Vernon, New Jersey

CHAPTER TWO

What is the first piece of advice you would give to your own child about getting into college?

Demonstrated interest is becoming more and more popular among colleges as a way to make sure the students they accept will likely attend (which impacts yield), as well as whether he should get scholarships/financial aid.

Robert Bardwell
Secondary-Level Vice President, American School Counselor Association
President, New England Association for College Admission Counseling
School Counselor and Director of Guidance & Student Support Services
Monson High School
Monson, Massachusetts

Decide who you want to be before you decide where you want to go: the best applications are from applicants who have interests that truly match the strength of a school.

Mandee Adler
Founder and Principal
International College Counselors
Hollywood, Florida

Students need to understand that colleges look at grades mostly from 9th to 11th grade.

Valerie Simmons, MEd
School Counselor
Pennsylvania

Don't worry about the price tag of the school at first; we'll work on the finances later.

Livia Sklar
Guidance Counselor
Bronx Aerospace Academy High School
Bronx, New York

For students who are weaker academically, applying early can be the difference between getting accepted or rejected by a college.

Valerie Simmons, MEd
School Counselor
Pennsylvania

While most students are anxious about getting into college, most colleges are equally anxious about getting students.

Philip M. Kavanagh
District Director of Guidance and Counseling
Lakeland Central School District
Shrub Oak, New York

The last thing a college applicant should do is frantically start joining clubs and doing activities in his or her junior year—by then it's too late.

Scott Shrum
Co-Author
Your MBA Game Plan:
Proven Strategies for Getting into the Top Business Schools
Director of MBA Admissions Research
Veritas Prep
Malibu, California

Kids today are deluged with mail from hundreds of schools. They're solicited by colleges as early as ninth grade. It's important for them to realize that colleges are businesses that are looking for customers, so the kids need to be savvy consumers.

Livia Sklar
Guidance Counselor
Bronx Aerospace Academy High School
New York, New York

College rankings do not promise a better college experience, competitive career placements, or higher salaries.

Lisa McDonald
Counselor
Chicago, Illinois

The college search journey has to be self-driven. Parents and counselors can and should be a resource for the young adult, but the force behind the search cannot be external.

William Slocum
Guidance Counselor
Lenape High School
Medford, New Jersey

Most students can be happy at either a big or a small school. Often, at the end of the process, when students are trying to decide which place to go, size is not an important factor. It's that "gut feeling" that one has when on a particular campus that usually determines the choice.

Betsy Sherwood
Guidance Counselor
Tappan Zee High School
Orangeburg, New York

"Getting into college" starts in 9th grade. That's when to start working to your potential and identifying your intellectual and extracurricular passions.

Lora K. Block, MA, CEP
Independent Educational Consultants Association
Bennington, Vermont

Learning to enjoy the college admissions process, not just "survive" it, totally changes the dynamics in very positive ways. I believe it can also change the outcome.

Ronna Morrison
Independent Educational Consultants Association
Ronna Morrison Associates
Demarest, New Jersey

Begin your high school career taking the most challenging courses that are offered in your high school and that are appropriate for your academic abilities, and continue that through your senior year.

The transcript is the most important part of the application.

Farron Goddell Peatross, MA, CEP
Independent Educational Consultants Association
Memphis, Tennessee

Hard work works! If you have a strong work ethic, your success is enhanced in every area of your life. Regardless of your intellectual abilities, the ability to work hard enriches your life and opens doors to college opportunities.

Keith Elmore
Counselor for Gifted Students
Liberty High School
Liberty, Missouri

Where you go matters if you know who you are and what you want before you go.

Keith Berman, CEP
President
Options for College, Inc.
New York, New York

If it feels good and it has what you want, go for it.

Don Dietrich
Director of College Guidance
Tower Hill School
Wilmington, Delaware

Don't forsake your passion(s) at the expense of your academics. Become a student of what you love.

Jessica Sharkey, MEd
College Pathways of Arizona
Arizona

Do not place emphasis on a college's name; instead, evaluate the academic offerings of the school and remember what is most important is what *you* do with the four years you spend in college.

Marilyn G.S. Emerson, MSW, CEP
Independent Educational Consultants Association
College Planning Services, Inc.
Chappaqua, New York

Making the location of a school of primary importance may make someone miss some wonderful place that would be perfect for them.

Betsy Sherwood
Guidance Counselor
Tappan Zee High School
Orangeburg, New York

The important thing is to find a school that empowers you and helps you grow as a scholar and as an individual.

Cristiana M. Quinn, MEd
College Admission Advisors, LLC
Providence, Rhode Island

Do what makes you happy. Don't base your college choices on what makes your parents happy or on where your friends are going. Find the school that is right for you based on your choice of major and the college demographics that work for you.

Jennifer Muffick
School Counselor
J.I. Case High School
Racine, Wisconsin

Choosing the right classes—a challenging curriculum but one where you can still maintain good grades—and taking your studies seriously begins in ninth grade. Most ninth graders, having just left junior high, do not have college on their minds.

Janet Rosier
Professional Member
Independent Educational Consultants Association and
Higher Education Consultants Association
Woodbridge, Connecticut

Students today are so over programmed that they become automatons, often unable to eat without verifying they have five minutes to spare between jazz flute and baton-twirling lessons. This scheduling frenzy causes many students to lose focus on what their true passions are. In so doing, they seek a college that will provide them with the inside track to the good life rather than an environment that provides opportunities to develop their established interests and create new ones.

Heath Einstein
Associate Director of College Counseling
The Hockaday School
Dallas, Texas

You may find that a gap year helps you get into the college you could not get into before! No college classroom can teach responsibility, accountability, time management, team building, and leadership skills like a year in a service-related gap-year program can. A gap-year program can perhaps lend a helping hand to the student in deciding what major they would like to pursue and build bridges toward internship opportunities during college and job networking after college.

Nathan J. Heltzel
School Counselor
Briarcliff High School
Briarcliff Manor, New York

Go to orientation. This is where you are taken on a tour of the campus by students, meet an advisor, sign up for classes, and learn many of the particulars of that university about financial aid, work study, and on- and off-campus housing. I know orientations seem to come at a time when many seniors feel overwhelmed by other factors in their life, but it is an important part of the transition from high school to college.

Steve Craig
Coconino High School
Flagstaff, Arizona

CHAPTER THREE

What is the one piece of advice you've given that's worked best for people?

The college process is similar to doing research. Start with the student's profile, build a list of possibilities based on several questions, and begin researching by attending college visits and information sessions. The final college list should include colleges that meet the student's profile.

Connect with graduates who are attending the colleges of interest. Spend a weekend at the college and go to classes. Get organized with a folder for each of the schools and build a list of pros and cons you can refer to.

Deborah Hardy, EdD
Chairperson of Guidance and Counseling Department
Irvington School District
Irvington, New York

The earlier a student can begin with his/her college planning, the less stress he/she will have.

Mandee Adler
Founder and Principal
International College Counselors
Hollywood, Florida

Ask what it is about high school that you liked or didn't like or what you would change about high school if you could. Then find a college that fits that response.

Joseph A. DeFrancesco, MA
Counselor
Council Rock High School–North
Newton, Pennsylvania

I caution my students to make sure that they aren't solely focused on their "reach" colleges and that they make sure they like the colleges that are targets for them. It is important not to put all of your emotional energy into just the reaches.

Janet Rosier
Professional Member
Independent Educational Consultants Association and
Higher Education Consultants Association
Woodbridge, Connecticut

Develop an expertise in a particular area that distinguishes you and that you have a strong affinity for. Demonstrate leadership in that field in your on-campus and off-campus extracurricular activities throughout high school. Highly competitive colleges want DEPTH in an interesting passion, not breadth in ordinary pursuits.

Cristiana M. Quinn, MEd
College Admission Advisors, LLC
Providence, Rhode Island

Get your testing in order early (finished by the end of junior year).

Philip M. Kavanagh
District Director of Guidance and Counseling
Lakeland Central School District
Shrub Oak, New York

The myth of the "one perfect college." Students spend much time trying to find the "one" school that is perfect. Students need to have an open mind and visit schools that only seem mildly interesting. It's amazing how these often turn out to be diamonds in the rough for the student.

Sandra K. Moore
Director of Guidance
Mount Saint Joseph Academy
Flourtown, Pennsylvania

We work a great deal on the personal statement that many colleges, scholarship agencies, and admission departments require as part of the application process. I have had many seriously talented students who wrestled with these essays, trying to outwit, out-cute, and impress in ways not always representative of the student. Depending on the prompt, we strive to help our students come up with an essay that truly represents their unique "voice," that displays their passion and self-motivation in whatever arena that passion exists. A well-written paper that honestly presents a picture of this person is more memorable than another long-winded rush of hyperbole.

Steve Craig
Coconino High School
Flagstaff, Arizona

An informed choice is a wise choice.

Jennifer Muffick
School Counselor
J.I. Case High School
Racine, Wisconsin

I work with many student athletes who want to play Division II varsity sports. I always tell them to determine if a campus would make them happy if they decided to quit their sport or if they were injured and could not play.

Jessica Sharkey, MEd
College Pathways of Arizona
Arizona

Bite your tongue on the college tour. This is your kid's chance to absorb, perceive, and form a subjective opinion.

Kris Hintz
Owner
Position U 4 College, LLC
New Vernon, New Jersey

Keep the college list to yourself! Personal success is completely appropriate to share after an acceptance has been offered. However, should they not get in, they oftentimes feel personal failure. They don't need the additional responsibility of explaining to family and friends why they did not get in.

Nathan J. Heltzel
School Counselor
Briarcliff High School
Briarcliff Manor, New York

Open your mind to learning about and discovering great schools that you or your parents might not know about already.

Howard Verman
Strategies For College, Inc.
Shelburne, Vermont

Money used to be the topic that was whispered about in the corner, many feeling shame for using cost as a determining factor as to where to go to college. Those days are gone.

Betsy Sherwood
Guidance Counselor
Tappan Zee High School
Orangeburg, New York

Be real. Applicants so often whip themselves into such a frenzy about presenting themselves as the "perfect applicant." What they don't realize is that who they are in real life is often closer to what those schools look for than the bland persona they end up putting into their applications.

Scott Shrum
Co-Author
Your MBA Game Plan:
Proven Strategies for Getting into the Top Business Schools
Director of MBA Admissions Research
Veritas Prep
Malibu, California

"Why do you want to go here?" To colleges, that is the most important question. Colleges want students most who also want them. Mention specifics on the college that show that you want to go there and that you have done your research on that institution. Mention professors whom you'd like to do research with (and what exactly it is about their research that fascinates you), clubs and organizations that the college has that you'd like to get involved in (and which one of their most recent events caught your eye), and specifics about their campus and programs that show them that, no matter how hard you tried, you could not recycle that essay and send it to another college because it was written exclusively for them.

Paul C. Kaser
College and Career Specialist
Bergen County Academies
Hackensack, New Jersey

Their last-choice safety school has to be someplace that they'd be happy to be if they had to be there for a year before they could transfer.

Deborah Shames
Independent College Search Consultant
Upper Saddle River, New Jersey

I always tell my students to start their search by visiting colleges that are nearby, even if they are not interested in attending these colleges. By making these early visits, students are then able to make intelligent decisions about the size or location of a school.

William Slocum
Guidance Counselor
Lenape High School
Medford, New Jersey

Visit, visit, and visit! You can't understand the culture of a college unless you've explored it in depth.

Judy Zodda
Zodda College Services
Framingham, Massachusetts

It is important to plan ahead, take plenty of time, and try to enjoy this process.

Robert Bardwell
Secondary-Level Vice President, American School Counselor
Association President, New England Association for College
Admission Counseling
School Counselor and Director of Guidance & Student
Support Services
Monson High School
Monson, Massachusetts

I tell all of my students they need to cultivate a relationship with the people who review their applications. In several instances, this, I firmly believe, was the difference between a student being admitted or denied admission to his or her desired college.

Heath Einstein
Associate Director of College Counseling
The Hockaday School
Dallas, Texas

This process should be one of empowerment. Each student should, without a doubt, feel as if they are in complete control of the college-planning process. Planning for college is about learning the steps, the processes, and the timing of all the necessary components.

Jean Marie Buckley, MEd, MPA
Founder and President
Buckley Educational Group, LLC
Burlingame, California

I have my students work over the summer and have their essays and common application complete before school starts in September of senior year.

Emilie Hinman
Dunbar Educational Consultants
New Canaan, Connecticut

Be honest when applying. Tell them why you're different.

Kristina L. Dooley
Independent Educational Consultant
Estrela Consulting
São Paulo, Brazil

Even if you are applying early decision, you should have all your other applications completed before December 10th.

Marilyn G.S. Emerson, MSW, CEP
Independent Educational Consultants Association
College Planning Services, Inc.
Chappaqua, New York

Weigh the pros and cons. Make your spreadsheet with all the details. Talk to friends, family, and ex students, but ultimately it is YOUR decision; not mine, not your parents' or your significant other's. Go with your heart after using your head, and trust your instincts!

Elisabeth Marksteiner
College Counselor & Alumni Relations
International School of Zug and Luzern
Zug, Switzerland

Merit money, scholarships that are offered to students who excel and usually exceed the usual level of competitiveness at one particular school, is being used to lure top students to schools that might not usually make their list. These opportunities should be considered seriously, as they often can provide wonderful opportunities for students.

Betsy Sherwood
Guidance Counselor
Tappan Zee High School
Orangeburg, New York

The most powerful and effective personal
statements are rooted in personal experiences
and are not mere narratives of them. In a concise,
detailed paragraph, tell me about your service trip
or the untimely death of a loved one. Then, unpack
the experience by explaining what you learned from
it and how it changed you and your worldview.
If possible, connect the wisdomgained from this
experience to your personal, college, or career goals.

Lisa McDonald
Counselor
Chicago, Illinois

Only apply to colleges where you'll be happy.

Livia Sklar
Guidance Counselor
Bronx Aerospace Academy High School
Bronx, New York

Apply to many tiers so you don't have many tears.

Nicole Oringer, MA, MEd
Partner
Ivy Educational Services
Scotch Plains, New Jersey

Shine where you shine. Don't struggle in your struggle. Know thyself!

Robert F. Kennedy
Counselor/Post-Grad Coordinator
Smoky Hill High School
Aurora, Colorado

Appreciate who you are and that you have gifts. Don't beat yourself up over a B or a lower SAT or ACT score...grades do not tell the whole story of you.

Cynthia Ann Markoch
IB Counselor
Eastside High School
Gainesville, Florida

CHAPTER FOUR

*What do students have to do
differently today from one year ago,
in terms of college admissions?*

The trends of college admissions have changed, but it is the realistic research of what matches the student that can make the outcome a good one.

Deborah Hardy, EdD
Chairperson of Guidance and Counseling Department
Irvington School District
Irvington, New York

Students must be as authentic as possible. Don't present an application that you think admission officers want to see—be yourself!

Jeannie Borin, MEd
President
College Connections
Encino, California

Don't use the term "safety school," but instead, "scholarship-likely school." It is amazing how this subtle change in attitude leads to a more motivated effort in applying to all schools.

Keith Berman, CEP
President
Options for College, Inc.
New York, New York

Apply early to as many schools as possible, and be prepared to receive several waitlist responses that may drag into summer, and pursue those avidly if you want an acceptance at those schools.

Cristiana M. Quinn, MEd
College Admission Advisors, LLC
Providence, Rhode Island

In general, I really see students giving a long, hard look at community colleges and whether or not that option can still serve them well to meet their long-term academic goals. As tuition of four-year universities climbs, scholarship dollars evaporate and out-of-state students look more pleasing (along with their out-of-state tuition) to a university, I am asking many of my undecided seniors who are financially strapped to consider the community colleges as a possibility.

Steve Craig
Coconino High School
Flagstaff, Arizona

Really understand each college's financial offer and its future implications.

Howard Verman
Strategies For College, Inc.
Shelburne, Vermont

The rule of thumb that applicants usually went by used to be "Go to the best school that you get into," but now it's evolved towards "Go to the best school that will cost a reasonable amount."

Scott Shrum
Co-Author
Your MBA Game Plan:
Proven Strategies for Getting into the Top Business Schools
Director of MBA Admissions Research
Veritas Prep
Malibu, California

They need to be sure to include a "financial safety school." In these tough times, families need to discuss the realities of going into debt to finance a $50K/year school that may or may not do a great job of helping their child get an education and, ultimately, a great job.

Deborah Shames
Independent College Search Consultant
Upper Saddle River, New Jersey

Look outside the box.

Nathan J. Heltzel
School Counselor
Briarcliff High School
Briarcliff Manor, New York

Students today need to be more technologically savvy than one year ago. Students are applying for admission and financial aid via technology in record numbers.

Robert Bardwell
Secondary-Level Vice President, American School Counselor
Association President, New England Association for College
Admission Counseling
School Counselor and Director of Guidance & Student
Support Services
Monson High School
Monson, Massachusetts

It is important that safety schools also be colleges that the student would like to attend, since it is possible that they will in fact be attending.

Todd Johnson
College Admissions Partners
Minnetonka, Minnesota

If there is one thing that continues to be true over time, it's the fact that kids have to feel in control of their ultimate choice. If parents insist that they know best, or if they make their choice of the "right" school the focus of the search, the road to disaster beckons. Even if students end up not happy at a particular college, they are in control of what happens next. They can own their decision, and take the next steps to find a good solution. If their parents made the ultimate choice for them, then blame takes up most of the room in trying to fix the problem.

Betsy Sherwood
Guidance Counselor
Tappan Zee High School
Orangeburg, New York

The great equalizer in this admissions game is the almighty dollar. With the current (and projected short-term) state of the economy, power lies with those who have the money to pay for college. Students need to align themselves with the right-fit school, not only in qualitative terms (access to faculty, living and learning communities, vegetarian options, etc.), but in quantitative terms (financial aid and merit scholarships) as well. Colleges are more likely to freeze employee salaries than limit financial aid because they need clients (students) to stay in business, so there is money out there.

Heath Einstein
Associate Director of College Counseling
The Hockaday School
Dallas, Texas

A student may have to look at colleges outside of their geographic comfort zone or colleges where they are truly a big fish in the applicant pool. This might ensure that they stand out, and get some "merit" money in addition to any financial aid they may qualify for.

Kiersten A. Murphy, MEd
Murphy College Consultants, LLC
Seattle/Bellevue, Washington

Today, students really have to understand *why* a college or university is a good fit for them. They need to be able to communicate that effectively when asked on their application (or during an interview).

Jessica Sharkey, MEd
College Pathways of Arizona
Arizona

The difference this year has to be based on the economy and the impact it has overall on their final choice of colleges. "Show me the money" has a much bigger role this year as compared to last year. As a result, the stress surrounding the opportunities for your final choice is more limited for students in general, but especially for public school students with middle-class incomes. They do not have the same options for need-based monies. Regardless of the programs now coming from the government, there are always students who don't benefit from these programs.

Keith Elmore
Counselor for Gifted Students
Liberty High School
Liberty, Missouri

Kids have to apply to more colleges today because of the uncertainty of admission decisions.

Don Dietrich
Director of College Guidance
Tower Hill School
Wilmington, Delaware

Have an interview with the admissions office and practice the face-to-face conversations ahead of time.

Deborah Hardy, EdD
Chairperson of Guidance and Counseling Department
Irvington School District
Irvington, New York

Students today need to be more technologically savvy than one year ago. They must be able to navigate the Internet and use all of the associated aspects of technology—chat, file sharing, social networks, etc. We are quickly becoming a paperless society and college admission will be no different.

Robert Bardwell
Secondary-Level Vice President, American School Counselor Association
President, New England Association for College Admission Counseling
School Counselor and Director of Guidance & Student Support Services
Monson High School
Monson, Massachusetts

Students have to be aware of the political and economic climate. They need to understand that the state of affairs in our nation is without precedence. And, this era is one of growth and one of change. I tell my students that as they move through this process and move on to their collegiate education, they are going to be part of the solution and part of the change in the years ahead.

Jean Marie Buckley, MEd, MPA
Founder and President
Buckley Educational Group, LLC
Burlingame, California

Students have to be more careful this year regarding online activities. It seems that admission officers, in greater numbers, are starting to pay more attention to the MySpace, Facebook, blogging, tweeting generation. It is more important than ever that students safeguard their online reputations.

William Slocum
Guidance Counselor
Lenape High School
Medford, New Jersey

Difficult economic times are causing more families to seek financial aid. I impress upon students a sense of duty to do their part as well: specifically, students should be applying for as many scholarships as possible and acting responsibly in their personal spending.

Lisa McDonald
Counselor
Chicago, Illinois

In an admissions committee meeting, you want your admissions representatives to stand up and say, "This kid is different. He will contribute to our college in a way no one else can."

Paul C. Kaser
College and Career Specialist
Bergen County Academies
Hackensack, New Jersey

Today, even more than last year, students have to be aware of the "business of college." Because of these economic times, admissions rates may tilt to their advantage. Your "reach" may be in reach.

Robert F. Kennedy
Counselor/Post-Grad Coordinator
Smoky Hill High School
Aurora, Colorado

CHAPTER FIVE

Do you have a tip that includes an SAT word?

I would share with parents the importance of *abdicating* their vision of the college process. Instead, *denote* what is important for the parent in the process of selecting college through a common dialogue.

Deborah Hardy, EdD
Chairperson of Guidance and Counseling Department
Irvington School District
Irvington, New York

Review the *prospectus* of any college in which you are interested and be prepared to ask a few questions on a visit or during an interview.

Jeannie Borin, MEd
President
College Connections
Encino, California

A *tersely* worded *vignette* is the key to the personal statement.

Keith Berman, CEP
President
Options for College, Inc.
New York, New York

Treat your college search as a *philonoist* would; rely on firsthand information rather than speculation.

Cristiana M. Quinn, MEd
College Admission Advisors, LLC
Providence, Rhode Island

Students today need to be *opportunistic* in the college admission process.

Livia Sklar
Guidance Counselor
Bronx Aerospace Academy High School
Bronx, New York

When making your list of potential colleges to apply to, don't be *ostentatious*! Pick a school because it is a good fit for you, not because of the name brand.

Nathan J. Heltzel
School Counselor
Briarcliff High School
Briarcliff Manor, New York

Colleges are not looking for *dilettantes*; they are seeking students with passion and initiative.

Howard Verman
Strategies For College, Inc.
Shelburne, Vermont

Your application should have heavy doses of *verisimilitude.* Keep it real throughout your application.

Scott Shrum
Co-Author
Your MBA Game Plan:
Proven Strategies for Getting into the Top Business Schools
Director of MBA Admissions Research
Veritas Prep
Malibu, California

To assume that a perfect SAT score is all you need to get into the college of your dreams would be *erroneous!*

Paul C. Kaser
College and Career Specialist
Bergen County Academies
Hackensack, New Jersey

To follow the *byzantine* logic of the SAT, separate the problem into manageable parts.

Nicole Oringer, MA, MEd
Partner
Ivy Educational Services
Scotch Plains, New Jersey

Beware of Facebook photos or comments that show you *carousing* with your friends. That might come back to haunt you.

Lora K. Block, MA, CEP
Independent Educational Consultants Association
Bennington, Vermont

The college-planning process can feel *daunting*, but change that emotion into one of *exuberance*!

Jean Marie Buckley, MEd, MPA
Founder and President
Buckley Educational Group, LLC
Burlingame, California

Should they apply early decision to one college, they should not neglect their applications to their secondary colleges or those to which they will be applying regular decision. I am *adamant* that they begin to work on those applications two weeks after the early decision application has been sent. This way, they will be able to enjoy their vacation.

Emilie Hinman
Dunbar Educational Consultants
New Canaan, Connecticut

Read *voraciously* on a *plethora* of topics to acquire the *erudition* requisite for college acceptances.

Elissa Sommerfield
Independent Educational Consultation Association
School Placement Services
Dallas, Texas

Be *audacious* in your effort and authentic in your heart.

Robert F. Kennedy
Counselor/Post-Grad Coordinator
Smoky Hill High School
Aurora, Colorado

CHAPTER SIX

Pearls of wisdom

It takes a family.

Steven Roy Goodman, MS, JD
Co-Author
College Admissions Together: It Takes a Family
Educational Consultant and Admissions Strategist
Washington, D.C.

Many colleges do not have well-known names, but have produced excellent students who go on to do great things either in the workplace or graduate school.

Cynthia Ann Markoch
IB Counselor
Eastside High School
Gainesville, Florida

Go to college fairs if you are able to.

Valerie Simmons, MEd
School Counselor
Pennsylvania

The ability to overcome adversity is a strong and positive personality characteristic.

Don Dietrich
Director of College Guidance
Tower Hill School
Wilmington, Delaware

Clean up e-mails and social networking profiles (being professional is essential).

Deborah Hardy, EdD
Chairperson of Guidance and Counseling Department
Irvington School District
Irvington, New York

In writing your essay, clarity is the equivalent of uniqueness. Applicants who are understood in a cohesive manner get in.

Keith Berman, CEP
President
Options for College, Inc.
New York, New York

The biggest mistake that educators and parents make is telling students that "junior year is the most important year for college." In reality, cumulative GPA and extracurricular participation is two-thirds set by the end of sophomore year.

Cristiana M. Quinn, MEd
College Admission Advisors, LLC
Providence, Rhode Island

Once your acceptances are in, pick up the phone and call the financial aid offices in the schools to which you've been accepted and try and make the best deal for yourself.

Livia Sklar
Guidance Counselor
Bronx Aerospace Academy High School
Bronx, New York

Something to remember is that getting in is a relative grain of sand; how students perform once in college is far more important.

Philip M. Kavanagh
District Director of Guidance and Counseling
Lakeland Central School District
Shrub Oak, New York

The college process isn't about acceptance: it's about choice. Learning how to choose is one of the great rites of passage on the way to autonomous adulthood. A fork in the road can be a welcome opportunity to learn about oneself. Decision making defines us.

Kris Hintz
Private Career and College Coach
Position U 4 College, LLC
New Vernon, New Jersey

Have a folder for every college you visit and take notes immediately after your visit, noting specific programs you liked. This will be particularly helpful when you are writing that college's supplement months later and answering the question "Why this college?"

Howard Verman
Strategies For College, Inc.
Shelburne, Vermont

I always encourage students to address any blemishes on their record (a low grade or a bad semester, a string of absences, a disciplinary issue, etc.) in a letter of explanation. Briefly explain what caused the issue at hand. Admissions counselors are people too, and they understand that situations beyond your control can and will affect your performance in school. If bad judgment or poor decision making was a factor, explain how you've grown from the experience, such that you won't make the same mistakes in college. Don't cross your fingers and hope that an admissions counselor might overlook the bad semester if you don't acknowledge it—it almost never happens.

Lisa McDonald
Counselor
Chicago, Illinois

Don't procrastinate!! Get as many of your essays as possible done over the summer so you can focus on your coursework in senior year!

Deborah Shames
Independent College Search Consultant
Upper Saddle River, New Jersey

Use all of the online tools available for researching colleges to see if you want to visit.

Judy Zodda
Zodda College Services
Framingham, Massachusetts

At the end of the day, one's health and happiness is far more important than whether or not one gets into a "tier one" school.

Heath Einstein
Associate Director of College Counseling
The Hockaday School
Dallas, Texas

Knowing how college admissions works is the first step to having a positive experience when you are going through it.

Paul C. Kaser
College and Career Specialist
Bergen County Academies
Hackensack, New Jersey

Each family should do an affordability assessment before the student sends in his or her applications, to be sure that "financial safety" colleges are on the list.

Lora K. Block, MA, CEP
Independent Educational Consultants Association
Bennington, Vermont

Colleges seem to be doing what they want to do. They admit who they want and deny those they don't want; many times there seems to be no rhyme or reason. Try very hard not to take it personally if you were an appropriate candidate!

Emilie Hinman
Dunbar Educational Consultants
New Canaan, Connecticut

Carve out time each week to discuss college.

Heath Einstein
Associate Director of College Counseling
The Hockaday School
Dallas, Texas

Prepare for college interviews by learning about the school you will be interviewing for and thinking about what you want the interviewer to know about you.

Marilyn G.S. Emerson, MSW, CEP
Independent Educational Consultants Association
College Planning Services, Inc.
Chappaqua, New York

The goal is to be happy and successful.

Elisabeth Marksteiner
College Counselor & Alumni Relations
International School of Zug and Luzern
Zug, Switzerland

Research scholarship opportunities within the different departments and colleges at the university you apply to. Available student aid varies greatly depending on what degree program and college you choose to enter.

Jennifer Muffick
School Counselor
J.I. Case High School
Racine, Wisconsin

Proof. Proof. Proof. A second or third set of eyes can do wonders for proofing an application.

Kristina L. Dooley
Independent Educational Consultant
Estrela Consulting
São Paulo, Brazil

Make the admission office remember you...not the alums you know nor the politicians that your parents voted for...but YOU. Since interviews are essentially a thing of the past, it is incumbent upon students to use the essay as effectively as possible. It remains one of the few items in an admission file over which the students still have control.

Don Dietrich
Director of College Guidance
Tower Hill School
Wilmington, Delaware

The selectivity of the school does not necessarily equate with the quality of the education the student will get there.

Deborah Shames
Independent College Search Consultant
Upper Saddle River, New Jersey

Be involved in a few things fully instead of 10 things just a bit.

Cynthia Ann Markoch
IB Counselor
Eastside High School
Gainesville, Florida

Students must pay attention to instinctual feelings when making decisions about their independence and educational path.

Jean Marie Buckley, MEd, MPA
Founder and President
Buckley Educational Group, LLC
Burlingame, California

You cannot describe the entire beach of your life; it is challenging enough to describe a grain of sand.

Keith Berman, CEP
President
Options for College, Inc.
New York, New York

Diversify your college search. Look at large, medium, small, private, and public. Look in the Midwest! Great deals on the Great Plains.

Robert F. Kennedy
Counselor/Post-Grad Coordinator
Smoky Hill High School
Aurora, Colorado

Get an advisor and become well acquainted with that person.

Steve Craig
Coconino High School
Flagstaff, Arizona

The truth is that only the top 20 or so schools have extremely low acceptance rates. Don't trick yourself into panicking and thinking that you won't get into a great college. There are far more than 20 great schools out there, and if you choose the right programs and put enough effort into researching these programs, the odds are that you will get into at least one of them.

Scott Shrum
Co-Author
Your MBA Game Plan:
Proven Strategies for Getting into the Top Business Schools
Director of MBA Admissions Research
Veritas Prep
Malibu, California

It is extremely easy to get caught up in all the frenzy that college admissions has become. It is crucial to understand that not getting accepted to your dream college does not mean that now your whole life is somehow going to be less than it would have been if you had been accepted. A good portion of your college experience will be what you decide to make it—and that can happen wherever you go.

Janet Rosier
Professional Member
Independent Educational Consultants Association and
Higher Education Consultants Association
Woodbridge, Connecticut

CHAPTER SEVEN

Parting advice

From a student

"There is a right college for everybody." That's what they say. But with thousands of colleges in the U.S. alone, how is anybody supposed to find the right one? Here's how I did:

For me, it really started sophomore year, when I almost accidentally visited my first university. I was at the Providence train station with over an hour before my train was supposed to arrive, so I took a self-guided tour around a nearby campus. It ended up becoming my "dream school", and I have not felt this way about any other university since. At the beginning of my junior year, I started considering different schools in different areas of the U.S. I began my technical search on CollegeClickTV.com, a website where I could compare and contrast different schools, read about them, and even watch uncensored videos made by current students. After doing intensive searches on this website, I formed a very tentative list of colleges I thought I might be interested in visiting, many of which were in the Northeast.

During winter break (February), I did my first round of visits. The best piece of advice about visiting schools I can give is to really observe—watch and listen—during your tour and info session. Taking notes and pictures may seem silly and unnecessary in the moment, but notes and photos are extremely useful later in the process, when you're struggling to differentiate school A from school B. This is crucial. After visiting many schools, the cafeterias, classrooms, dorms, and quads often blend together. Notes and pictures can be excellent reminders of what you liked best about each school.

In addition, many supplemental essays to the common application (the most commonly used application for U.S. schools) inquire "Why School X?" or "What makes School X different, in your opinion?" Schools like to know what it is about them that you as a student and young person are drawn to. They also need to know that you have carefully considered them as an institution where you could spend the next four or so years of your life. Notes and pictures can help you remember details, so you can effectively articulate in an essay what makes a certain school a good fit for you. They can also help you prove to a school that you are really interested in going there.

In March, after these visits, I took the SAT for the first time. Then I made my second group of visits during spring break, with my dad and brother. I kept a rolling list of the schools I visited and after each visit, I did a little research on the school's website to figure out whether there would be appropriate programs and majors for me. At the end of my junior year, I rewrote my tentative list of schools to give to the teachers whom I wanted recommendations from.

The end of your junior year is probably the best time to request recommendations from teachers. Junior year, for me, was a year of immense growth academically. I took my first AP course, which was somewhat of a rude awakening, but which prepared me for my senior-year courses. The teachers I had during my junior year, in my opinion, were the ones most fit to describe me as a student to the colleges I planned to apply to because I undoubtedly worked my hardest that year. In addition, senior-year teachers often don't know enough about you come time for you to apply to schools. Sophomore teachers may know you well, but because many students grow a lot during junior year, it's wise to select two teachers from junior year to provide you with recommendations. In addition, asking teachers for recommendations at the end of your junior year is perfect because it gives them plenty of time to consider what they would like to say about you, look over your transcript, and reflect on your performance in their class that year.

And then came summer: the perfect time to organize your thoughts from the year and get a jump on the inevitable stress of fall. I used my summer to concentrate on the schoolwork for the AP courses I would be starting in the fall and to study for the ACT, a test I had never taken. Having researched the ACT and SAT, I decided I would try the ACT. This is because, when you take the SAT, you are often also required (but not by every school) to send in two SAT II (subject tests you take in the areas you choose) scores along with your SAT scores. When you take the ACT with the writing supplement (a short essay that serves as a fifth section to the four-section test), you are often exempt from taking any subject tests (but this is not always true, it is wise to check the requirements of each individual school). This is beneficial to some and not so much to others. For me, having (regrettably) taken no subject tests when I took the SAT, the ACT was a good option.

After doing last bits of research on the schools in which I was interested and comparing them, keeping different factors in mind such as programs offered, academics, college life, athletics, campus, and location, I made a final list of schools that I would be happy attending. This list included six "safety" schools (where I had a very good chance of being admitted), six "target" schools (where my academic performance would meet requirements, but where I was not guaranteed admittance), and six "reaches" (where it would be difficult for me to get in, but not completely out of the question). On this final list, I made sure that I had not included any schools that would not accept my ACT with writing supplement score in lieu of SAT and SAT II scores.

I then created an account on the Common Application website and began filling it out. I added my almost-finalized list of schools to the website (although about three of my desired schools were not listed there). I clicked each school on the website and copied and pasted their supplements into a separate document. A supplement is an essay on a topic that the individual schools make up and request that you send in. This is in addition to the essay required on the common application and varies from school to school. Some schools have no supplement and some have up to four. I began considering these essays and even writing them as early as August.

There is another important factor about the college search process that each teenager must remember: college is a privilege, it is not something that is guaranteed and it is not something that everyone is lucky enough to experience. Regardless of the name of the college, its price, its location, or its image in the eyes of the critical public, being able to attend one is an incredible educational gift that should not be taken for granted. While it is easy to get caught up in the day-to-day tasks required by the college search process, I really believe that the most pertinent piece of advice is: remember how fortunate you are to be able to attend college at all.

Whether or not you decide to apply early to any school, it is wise to prepare other applications, because there is nothing certain about the application process. I will apply this fall, after having tested a couple more times, and hope for the best, because once you send your applications in, that's all you can do. Wish me luck!

Cole Yaverbaum

From a parent

For us, it really started when our daughter was born! How would we possibly ever be able to pay for college? How did our parents pay for our college? Do you know how much this costs?! If I had written this book 18 months ago, my simple and seemingly brilliant answer would have been: Save with a 529 Plan from the day your child is born! We did. (The wonders of being type A planners.) But the world has changed a little in the past year and someone must have been laughing while we were planning. So we rethought our plan.

"There is a right college for everybody." Just like my daughter said. Her "right college" probably won't be the school I'd choose for her. Nor was mine, at that age, my parents' first choice for me. While I was a Penn State football fan, with a mother who was a lifelong professor there and a father who was an alumnus (and who still never misses a game), it was not the college I most wanted to go to. Thankfully, my parents quietly and respectfully watched me choose another direction. A different path. A path that was sometimes wrong, sometimes right, but always my path to own.

If you're reading this chapter and you're a parent, we can all relate: How did they grow up so fast? My dad was dropping me off for my freshman year at American University in Washington, D.C. just last month, wasn't he? He said his own emotional good-bye that I can only fully understand now. He knew that day was a crossroad for all of us. I picked my path. He went home.

During our daughter's college search, for the first time in our lives as parents, my wife and I were determined to be silent partners who gave advice and a dash of reality when appropriate. And by "appropriate," I mean when we were asked. Because we weren't choosing where to spend the next four years of *our* lives. We're staying home. We like our nest! And while our life's experiences are certainly of great value to our daughter, when she doesn't rely on us for all the answers, she learns lessons about life the same way we did: by experiencing them.

So while choosing a college was far too important a decision for our daughter to make without *any* of our insight and wisdom, we were determined to let her take charge and use her own judgment. Follow her own direction. Find her own path to own.

No matter what you have done the past 18 years to plan and save (or not), the time has officially come to understand the financial realities of higher education today. Colleges are more fiscally challenged than ever before in our lifetimes, and so are most families. That sounds like a real downer, but there can be a happy ending. There will be for us. I know that because I spent a lot of time with my daughter as we researched and wrote this book, quietly watching and enjoying her as she grew up quite a bit. I watched her invest the time and energy needed to make an educated, well-researched decision, and I got to tag along. By the way, because you may have forgotten, dorm rooms are very small!

While my daughter held up her end of the bargain as the Managing Partner of the search process, I made sure to hold up mine as the Chief Financial Officer, exploring all the options. The good news is that there are many. Be a good CFO and do your homework. Every situation is unique. Regardless of your roles and responsibilities in life, your income, your influence, your opinions, and your own personal comfort level, the college search process can be a really fun, enriching, and rewarding experience to cherish and embrace. Be a partner. Be interested. Impart a little wisdom. And don't miss the once-in-a-lifetime opportunity to be fully engaged at this particular crossroad of your child's life.

As I write this, I already know that, like many things in life, when we are long done, this will be one of those unique experiences I'll wish I could do again. So I'm thoroughly enjoying our partnership and my role. And on my daughter's graduation day, when I long to be back here again, I'll feel like I appreciated this time I spent with her. I recognized the significance of the crossroad. I accepted that she will leave the nest. And I loved every second of watching her choose a new, temporary nest where she'll stay until she decides what will follow at her next crossroad.

Eric Yaverbaum

Resources

College Timeline

Sophomore Year

➤ Maintain good grades

➤ Consider taking a subject test if possible

➤ Get involved in things you care about

➤ Pursue your hobbies

➤ Participate in local community service if possible

➤ Take the PSAT if your school offers it

➤ Develop a good relationship with your guidance counselor

Junior Year

➤ Continue to maintain good grades

➤ Challenge yourself in terms of your courses

➤ Retake the PSAT if your school offers it

➤ Continue the pursuit of your hobbies

➤ Continue volunteering when possible

➤ Research the colleges you may be interested in

➤ Maintain your relationship with your guidance counselor: visit frequently and communicate about your goals

September

➤ Research the SAT and ACT; decide which one seems right for you

➤ Begin preparing for the SAT and/or ACT

➤ Register for the October SAT and/or ACT if desired

October

➤ Continue to prepare for the SAT and/or ACT

➤ Take the October SAT and/or ACT if desired

➤ Consider making college visits over December break

December

➤ Make a few college visits if possible

➤ Register for the January SAT if desired

➤ Register for the February ACT if desired

➤ Consider what subjects you could later take a subject test in

January

➤ Take the January SAT if desired

February

➤ Take the February ACT if desired

➤ Register for the March SAT if desired

➤ Begin preparing for AP exams if applicable

March

➤ Take the March SAT if desired

➤ Register for the April ACT if desired

➤ Register for the May SAT and/or SAT II if desired

➤ Plan to visit colleges over spring break

April

➤ Register for the June SAT and/or SAT II if desired

➤ Go to college fairs if possible

➤ Begin noting the qualities you desire in a school

➤ Take notes during college visits and follow up with a "thank you"

➤ e-mail or letter following your visit

May

➤ Register for the June ACT if desired

➤ Take the May SAT and/or SAT II if desired

➤ Take AP exams if applicable

➤ Continue to work hard in your school courses

➤ Consider your summer goals

June

➤ Take the June ACT and/or SAT and/or SAT II

July/August

➤ Consider participating in community service

➤ Prepare for fall standardized tests if desired

➤ Consider doing a few more college visits

➤ Begin the common application and form a tentative list of colleges

➤ Register for the September ACT if desired

➤ Begin thinking about your college essay(s)

Senior Year

➤ Continue taking the most challenging courses for you

➤ Continue pursuing what interests you

➤ Continue to maintain good grades

September

➤ Meet with your guidance counselor to discuss future plans and look over your transcript

➤ Make a clear list of possible colleges that includes safeties, targets, and reaches; begin applications and write down deadlines

➤ Take the September ACT if desired

➤ Register for any fall standardized tests if desired (October or December ACT; October, November, or December SAT and/or SAT II)

➤ Check for college visits at your school

➤ Go to any information programs your school offers about college

➤ Ask at least two teachers with whom you have a good relationship for letters of recommendation

➤ Begin forming a resume

October

➤ Take October SAT and/or SAT II and/or ACT if desired

➤ Should you decide to apply early decision, finalize that application

➤ Attend interviews at your schools of interest if possible

➤ Consider financial aid and/or scholarship opportunities

➤ Finalize your college essay(s)

November

➤ Note the November early decision deadlines if applicable

➤ Take the SAT and/or SAT II if desired

➤ Communicate with your guidance counselor

➤ Finish college applications if applying regular decision

December

➤ Note the December regular decision deadlines if applicable

➤ If you are an early decision or rolling admission applicant, check the mail frequently for decisions regarding your admission

January

➤ Finalize your FAFSA (financial aid) form and submit it

➤ Go over your grades from the first semester

➤ Note the January regular decision deadlines if applicable

April

➤ Consider acceptance letters

➤ Make last visits to colleges you have been accepted to if you are still unsure and have not yet committed

May

➤ Note the May deadlines for committing to schools

➤ Commit to a college

➤ Tell the colleges that you have decided against of your decision

➤ In person or in a letter, thank the people who have assisted you in your college journey

➤ Take AP exams if applicable

➤ Maintain good grades

Financial Aid/Scholarships

1) http://www.fafsa.ed.gov/ — FAFSA (federal financial aid)

2) http://www.staffordloan.com/ — Stafford Loan (federal student loan)

3) http://www.parentplusloan.com/ — PLUS (parent loan program)

4) https://profileonline.collegeboard.com/prf/index.jsp — CSS financial aid profile

5) http://www.finaid.org/ — Financial aid guide

6) www.onlineschoolfinancialaid.com — Database of schools offering financial aid

7) www.estudentloan.com — Compare and search for student loans

8) www.iefa.org — Financial aid college scholarship search

9) http://studentaid.ed.gov/students/publications/student guide/index.html — Financial aid resource publications from the U.S. Department of Education

10) http://studentaid.ed.gov/ — Student aid on the Web

11) http://www.fastweb.com/ — Fastweb scholarship search

12) http://www.collegenet.com/mach25/app — Match 25 scholarship search

13) http://www.guaranteed-scholarships.com/ — Guaranteed scholarships

14) http://www.studentscholarshipsearch.com/ — Student scholarship search

15) http://www.scholarshipexperts.com/ — Scholarship experts

16) http://www.collegescholarships.org/ — College scholarships

17) http://apps.collegeboard.com/cbsearch_ss/welcome.jsp — College Board scholarship search

18) http://www.collegescholarships.com/free_scholarship_searches.htm — Free scholarship search

College Life

1) http://www.collegeclicktv.com/ — Thousands of student interviews

2) http://www.collegeclicktv.com/comparisons — College comparisons

3) http://www.collegeclicktv.com/top5 — Top-five lists

4) http://www.sparknotes.com/college/life/ — SparkNotes on your first year in college

5) http://www.mtv.com/ontv/dyn/college_life/series.jhtml — MTV show displaying *College Life* uncensored

6) http://collegelife.about.com/ — "Everything You Need to Know to Enjoy Your Time in College"

7) http://www.quintcareers.com/college_life.html — College Resources: Teen Life/College Life

8) http://www.collegeconfidential.com/college_life/index.html — College Confidential

Test Prep

1) http://www.collegeboard.com/ — College Board (SAT/ SAT II registration)

2) http://www.act.org/ — ACT registration

3) http://www.princetonreview.com/ — Princeton Review test preparation

4) http://www.ets.org/portal/site/ets/menuitem.3a88fea2 8f42ada7c6ce5a10c3921509/?vgnextoid=85b65784623f 4010VgnVCM10000022f95190RCRD — Educational Testing Service

5) http://www.kaptest.com/index.jhtml — Kaplan test preparation

6) http://www.collegeinsightstestprep.com/index.shtml — College Insights

7) http://huntingtonlearning.com/ — SAT/PSAT and ACT preparation

8) http://tutoring.sylvanlearning.com/index.cfm — Sylvan Learning Center (tutoring)

9) http://www.testprepreview.com/ — Free online practice test

Athletics

1) http://www.ncaa.org/wps/ncaa?key=/
   NCAA/Legislation+and+Governance/
   Eligibility+and+Recruiting/InformationforCollege-
   BoundStudent-Athletes — National Collegiate
   Athletic Association

2) http://www.collegecoachesonline.com/ — College
   coaches online

3) http://www.collegesportsscholarships.com/timeline.htm
   — Athletic scholarship timeline

4) http://www.college-athletic-scholarships.com/ —
   College athletic scholarships

Other Resources

1) https://www.commonapp.org/CommonApp/default.
   aspx — The common application

2) http://www.quintcareers.com/college_admissions/ —
   Answers to common college admission questions

3) http://college.sparknotes.com/ — SparkNotes college
   search

4) http://www.naviance.com/products-services/college-
   planner.html — College planner by Naviance

5) http://www.fiskeguide.com/ — Fiske Guide to Colleges

Sample College Essay

Letter to My Mother

"Tickle my back, Mommy." I couldn't sleep when I was younger. Instead, I conveniently placed myself between my two parents in their bed each night. I'd sleep with them, my back facing my mother so she could tickle it and whisper mock-ocean noises into my ear until I fell asleep. I was safe and comforted this way, between my two best friends.

In the city, we woke up together each morning. She would help me get dressed and comb my thin hair. We walked to school most days, my mom and I. Some days she'd carry me, some days she'd push me in my stroller, others I'd walk beside her. I knew she had Multiple Sclor-something at the time, but I wasn't really sure just what that meant. I remember one day she fell on our way to school, and I was scared; mommies aren't supposed to fall, I thought.

Having a baby, given her medical condition, was dangerous the doctor said; she did it anyway. Watching me hold him made it worth it. We moved to Larchmont when she gave birth to my brother, Jace. I remember she was apprehensive about taking care of two babies. "I'm not a baby, Mama. You take care of me, and I'll take care of the baby," I would tell her.

The last lucid image I have of her standing was on one of our first few days in our new home. I remember watching her walk up the stairs to our front porch, baby in arms. I secretly worried she might fall again, as the image had never left me. The transition she underwent from legs to a walker is blurred to me, but it must've happened because I remember coming home from school to her on her walker, struggling to move towards me only to kiss my forehead. The rest is difficult for me to discern, but over the next couple years, her walker became a wheelchair. Metal bars appeared throughout the house; on the walls, in the shower. She still took me to school, but not the same way; I sat on her lap as she drove her motorized scooter down the streets, waving at literally everyone we would pass. "Mommy, do you even KNOW them?" I'd always ask. No, she would shake her head smiling. Her optimism never ceased to captivate me.

The middle school was further, and I started walking there with friends. Every day she would ask how my day went, doing her best to remain a prominent part of my life, despite my inevitable increasing independence. As I got older and began going to high school, her health continued to deteriorate. No longer able to "sit her way" up the stairs, we made a bedroom for her downstairs. I started quizzing myself for tests; I could no longer rely on her for this because of her shaky hands, blurry vision, and sporadic memory loss. I began helping her get dressed and I began combing her thinning hair.

Despite the effect it has undeniably had on my life, her physical handicap has never fully cut off her ability to be an enduring and idealistic mother. She wrote a book for me, *Letters to My Daughter*, of all the things I said or did as a child that amazed her. She gave it to me on my sixteenth birthday. No matter how many times I read it, I am never anything but touched in the aftermath. With it I am, and always will be, able to remember the kind of person my mother is, the kind of person I hope to be.

I can tell when she watches me that so far I am fulfilling her expectations for me as a young person, not just by the vivid descriptions she has provided me with of my youth, but by the way she listens intently as I read her what I have written, asks me about my life, and absorbs all that I tell her. Whether she will remember these things tomorrow, or in a year from now, is questionable. That I will remember these things always is definite.

She used to complain when I slept in the bed with her that there wasn't enough room for three people in a small bed. I sleep in my own room now, but I think she misses me sleeping next to her. Sometimes I still do. She's older now, easily tired, but her soul is forever energetic. And she still tickles my back the same way.

Cole Yaverbaum

About the Authors

Cole Yaverbaum, age 17, is a student at Mamaroneck High School in Westchester County. A senior, Cole is currently in search of a college herself. She is a member of student council, the National Honor Society, and several other committees and clubs at her school. In her spare time she enjoys biking, reading, writing, and practicing piano. Although this is her first published book, she aspires to pursue her writing career in college.

Eric Yaverbaum co-founded Jericho Communications in 1985, the 11th ranked PR firm in the country to work for, and served as its president before its successful merger in

2005. He founded Ericho Communications in 2006 and the company now has offices in White Plains, New York City, and Tampa, Florida. Additionally, he currently serves as President of CollegeClickTV.com and is a co-founder of Tappening and ReadToVote.org.

He brings more than 25 years of experience to the practice of public relations and has earned a reputation for his expertise in strategic media relations, crisis communications, and media training. Eric has amassed extensive experience in counseling a wide range of clients in corporate, political, consumer, retail, technology, and professional services markets and in building brands such as Jose Cuervo, Smirnoff, Sony, TCBY, Tae Bo, Mrs. Fields, Subway Sandwiches, IKEA, Domino's Pizza, H&M, and American Express, among many others.

He is also a frequent talk-show guest on national and regional television and radio programs and networks, including *CBS This Morning*, *Today*, CNN, *Larry King Live*, *Your World with Neil Cavuto*, MSNBC, and CW11 and has been a regular on Fox News' *Strategy Room* since before the recent presidential election.

Eric wrote the best-selling book *I'll Get Back to You* (McGraw Hill). He is also the author of the first and second editions of *Public Relations For Dummies* (Wiley Books), which is required reading in marketing classes at 57 universities in the United States. His third book, *Leadership Secrets of the World's Most Successful CEOs* (Dearborn) has been translated into 13 languages. His last book, *Everything Leadership* (Adams), came out in May 2008.

Eric was an active member of the highly selective Young President's Organization for over a decade, where he was the Chapter Chairman in New York City. His widely acclaimed "Walk a Mile in My Shoes" campaign helped push increased spending on stem cell research through the House and led to his being named one of the heroes of the public relations industry by industry bible *PRWeek*. Eric currently sits on the board of advisers for the Accelerated Cure Project for Multiple Sclerosis, where he received the prestigious Water Cove Award in October of 2009.

BUY A SHARE OF THE FUTURE IN YOUR COMMUNITY

These certificates make great holiday, graduation and birthday gifts that can be personalized with the recipient's name. The cost of one S.H.A.R.E. or one square foot is $54.17. The personalized certificate is suitable for framing and will state the number of shares purchased and the amount of each share, as well as the recipient's name. The home that you participate in "building" will last for many years and will continue to grow in value.

Here is a sample SHARE certificate:

YES, I WOULD LIKE TO HELP!

I support the work that Habitat for Humanity does and I want to be part of the excitement! As a donor, I will receive periodic updates on your construction activities but, more importantly, I know my gift will help a family in our community realize the dream of homeownership. **I would like to SHARE in your efforts against substandard housing in my community!** *(Please print below)*

PLEASE SEND ME _____ SHARES at $54.17 EACH = $ $_____

In Honor Of: _____

Occasion: (Circle One)   HOLIDAY   BIRTHDAY   ANNIVERSARY

     OTHER: _____

Address of Recipient: _____

Gift From: _____ *Donor Address:* _____

Donor Email: _____

I AM ENCLOSING A CHECK FOR $ $_____ PAYABLE TO HABITAT FOR HUMANITY OR PLEASE CHARGE MY VISA OR MASTERCARD *(CIRCLE ONE)*

Card Number _____ Expiration Date: _____

Name as it appears on Credit Card _____ Charge Amount $ _____

Signature _____

Billing Address _____

Telephone # Day _____ Eve _____

PLEASE NOTE: Your contribution is tax-deductible to the fullest extent allowed by law.
Habitat for Humanity • P.O. Box 1443 • Newport News, VA 23601 • 757-596-5553
www.HelpHabitatforHumanity.org

Printed in the USA
CPSIA information can be obtained
at www.ICGtesting.com
JSHW082213140824
68134JS00014B/603

9 781600 377280